World War II

Following the Great War, or the "War to End All Wars," no one could have imagined that history would repeat itself just a few years later. With nearly the entire world slumped in an economic depression, nations were spiraling, as one by one, they raised tariffs and importation taxes in an effort to internalize their economies and benefit businesses in country. Unfortunately, isolation techniques–particularly in the U.S.– proved to be devastating for other nations whose economies depended on the nation's ability to export to other wealthier nations. This, in addition to some nations' lasting grudges and mixed feelings about the end results of the Great War, led to increased tensions and the constant threat of another outbreak of war.

Though many events have been cited as the cataclysmic incident that started the Second World War, it would be impossible to isolate one event as the sole instigator for the war. For one, the economic downturn following World War I made several countries desperate for solutions, including Germany and Japan. Germany, having been forced to sign the Treaty of Versailles, which severely limited its progress and demanded unrealistic payment for its involvement in the war, was left broke, suffering, and desperate for options. Japan, on the other hand, was severely economically devastated by the U.S.'s increased tariffs, preventing the nation from exporting to the number one country who imported Japanese goods. With the U.S. off the market, Japan's economy plummeted and the nation searched desperately for options, though the limited resources within the country's borders limited them. If Japan was going to be successful and save its economy, the Japanese would have to look outside their borders.

Table Of Contents

Japanese Invasion of Manchuria 4

The Rise of Adolf Hitler 10

The German-Soviet Nonaggression Pact 12

Dunkirk 15

The Battle of Britain 21

Pearl Harbor 26

The Destruction of Cologne 35

The Battle of Midway 41

The German Surrender at Stalingrad 47

Hiroshima Bomb 51

Conclusion 55

Sources 57

Japanese Invasion of Manchuria

With Japan's economic instability as one of the major factors motivating its search for new opportunities, Japan turned to its Asian neighbors for assistance. In addition to their economic crisis, the Japanese believed that intervening and protecting their neighboring countries was both a responsibility and an honor, and therefore was something they would not undertake lightly. Since the Japanese believed that their Emperor was a direct descendant of god, they considered their governmental and religious systems to be relevant to other nations outside of their own, making it Japan's duty to spread its culture and religious influence to the entire world. Believing themselves to be a holy race united under their father emperor, as well as acting as amalgamators and mediators of culture in Asia, the Japanese also felt it their responsibility to protect their neighboring countries from the communism that was overwhelming Russia and threatening to spill over its borders.

In addition, the Japanese especially believed that the Chinese were a similar but inferior race, requiring the guidance and care of the Japanese. Thus, war was considered an acceptable method for spreading religion and peace throughout the world, actually making world peace the ultimate result of war. With this ideology, the Japanese believed themselves to be the instigators of noble and purposeful wars, which would bring about peace and prosperity for all. In order to spread this belief, the Japanese worked hard to instill these ideas in the minds of all generations using intensive indoctrination and creating an unparalleled sense of nationalism among the people. With the installment of the Japanese language as the national language and the increase in loyalties to the Emperor, the Father of Japan, many of the Japanese believed in their expansion across Asia — and if they disagreed, there was no tolerance for questioning.

Additionally, some of Japan's own politics encouraged its invasion of other countries, primarily the increase in the people's trust of the military over the nation's politicians. After the humiliation of the first war, which left Japan wounded and in poor national standing, the Japanese were quick to accept the military's expansionist policy and the power that would come with it. Believing their nation to be the veritable economic equivalent of Great Britain, the Japanese had hoped to increase their national standing through the acquisition of colonies and external resources. Unfortunately, Japan did not have direct access to any colonies, leaving expansion through neighboring countries their only option. Additionally, since the Japanese suffered under the rule of various corrupt regimes for far too many years, they no longer believed in their politicians. With that in mind, the people greatly favored the military's plans for expansion over and above the government's diplomatic policy, especially considering their later distrust of the nation's politicians. This attitude especially increased when the naval general became one of the only legitimate members of staff to directly advise the throne, allowing the Japanese navy to undercut political decisions and significantly influence the people's opinions. Lastly, the Japanese were embittered toward western nations due to the racism they felt they experienced in political affairs. Unfortunately, many western nations felt the need to intervene in Japanese affairs in which they had no personal involvement, and continuously ignored the Japanese representatives in meetings of diplomacy. Thus, this increased Japan's need to better its national standing and become a powerful adversary in the world race for success.

With the people's vote of support and a religious purpose, Japan began to spread its tendrils throughout Asia, taking Korea, Taiwan, Okinawa, and China through the Sino-Japanese and Russo-Japanese wars. In their efforts to chase Russia out of Manchuria, the Japanese took the Southern Manchuria Railway, which both provided Japan with an incredible opportunity for economic development and allowed them to deploy their Kwantung army and acquire the Kwantung Territory. Once Japan took the Southern Manchuria Railway on September 18, 1932, Colonel Itagaki Selshior, having assumed Consul Morishima's position when the leader refused to act without diplomatic resolution, ordered the mobilization of the Kwantung army and the attack on Manchurian cities and Chinese military barracks. Though Japan advertised their takeover as beneficial for China, there was no denying the economic benefits that Japan gained from their invasion. Aside from providing Japan with useful railway services, Manchuria also provided Japan with some much-needed resources, which made the area a source of boundless potential and raw materials for Japan to exploit. In order to promote this mentality, the Japanese media promoted the message that Manchuria was acting as "Japan's lifeline," leading to even greater public support for the military efforts of "protecting Japanese interests." Additionally, taking over China and ensuring that the land would not fall into the hands of the USSR and its communist policy meant that both China and Japan would be more than safe from the influence of the Russians. Thrilled with their success, the Japanese immediately established outposts in China and prepared to settle into their new "colony."

Unfortunately, the Japanese quickly found that the Chinese were less than excited about Japan's interference in their lives. When Japan proposed 21 demands for China, which would effectively put the nation under Japanese rule, the Chinese were less than enthusiastic. Though the other world powers intervened and prevented China from falling under Japanese rule, the Chinese still limited their imports from Japan, which was a serious offense considering that China was one of Japan's major importers. Since the Chinese had no desire to be overtaken by their Japanese neighbors, they began acting out against them, expressing anti-Japanese sentiment through protesting, boycotting Japanese goods, and occasionally even acting out in violence against the Japanese staying in the nation. Additionally, Japan's actions directly violated the Kellogg-Briand Pact of August 27, 1928, which Japan signed as a part of its involvement with the League of Nations. Since the League of Nations decided not to allow Japan any slack for its invasion of Manchuria, the League continued to strictly regulate Chinese and Japanese activities and directly confronted Japan in regards to its latest invasion. The U.S. Government specifically called upon Japan to honor the policies of the Kellogg-Briand Pact, hoping to resolve the issue easily, but the Japanese government refused to concede. Though the Japanese responded that they intended to continue friendly relations with China and had no intention of invading Manchuria for their own national purpose, the movements of their military into the area and their manipulation of the resources there proved otherwise. In fact, Japan had effectively destroyed all remaining administrative authority of the government of the Chinese Republic in South Manchuria by the end of 1931, which had been operational until the Japanese invaded in September of that year.

With Japan effectively ignoring the demands of the League of Nations and lying about their position in China, the League grew more and more irritated with the Japanese government and some nations, particularly the U.S., decided it could not afford to work with the Japanese until they were compliant with the League's demands. The U.S. government officially stated that it would not work with the Chinese or Japanese governments as they were, in their current state, "nor did it intend to recognize any treaty or agreement entered into between these governments which might impair the treaty rights of the United States or its citizens in China; that it did not intend to recognize 'any situation, treaty, or agreement' which might be brought about by means contrary to the obligations of the Kellogg-Briand Pact." With Japan's economy threatened by the United States' decision to withhold trade with the nation, the Japanese government finally changed tactics and asked what they could do to remedy the situation and lift the ban on importation and exportation. The U.S., in response, stated that they would reinstate trade with the Chinese and the Japanese if, and only if, both governments adhered to the following conditions: "cessation of all acts of violence on both sides, no further preparation for hostilities, withdrawal of both Chinese and Japanese combatants in the Shanghai area, protection of the International Settlement at Shanghai by the establishment of neutral zones, and, upon acceptance of the foregoing, prompt negotiations to settle all outstanding controversies between Japan and China with the aid of neutral observers or participants" (U.S. Department of State Publication 1983). While China easily agreed to all of these policies, more than willing to comply with both the United States' and the League of Nations' demands, Japan was a bit more hesitant. Though the Japanese government was willing to comply with some of the points made, it flatly rejected the second and fifth conditions. Unfortunately, no agreement was ever made and the proposal ultimately came to nothing.

Then, in 1932, the U.S. Ambassador to Japan reported that the situation with Japan and Manchuria was growing more dire, since the Japanese military was working hard to strengthen the public's nationalism and encourage their people's distrust in and poor opinion of all nations outside their own. The U.S. Ambassador feared "that the Japanese military machine had been 'built for war', felt prepared for war, and would 'welcome war'; that it had never yet been beaten and possessed unlimited self-confidence." This statement was followed by the Japanese military extending their Manchurian borders in January of 1933, which increased concern regarding Japan's intentions for its newly acquired land. The League of Nations, meanwhile, was considering the Lytton Commission's report, which had been appointed to investigate and analyze the situation in Manchuria. The Commission reported that, "the military operations of the Japanese in Manchuria could not be regarded as measures of legitimate self-defense; that the regime which the Japanese had set up there disregarded the wishes of the people of Manchuria and was not compatible with the fundamental principles of existing international obligations." The League, left without much choice, found this report to be true and adopted it on February 24, 1933, which immediately resulted in the Japanese walking out of the assembly. Shortly thereafter, on March 27, 1933, Japan gave notice of its decision to leave the League of Nations, officially cutting its ties with the greater powers of the western world.

The Rise of Adolf Hitler

With most of the world's focus centered on the crisis in Asia, the German economy was left struggling, like several European nations, to survive the worldwide economic depression and the unattainable terms of the Treaty of Versailles. The Germans, devastated from their loss in the First World War and desperate for answers, turned to an unusually optimistic and charismatic leader who was coming to power: Adolf Hitler. Following his role as a German soldier in the Great War, Hitler found purpose and meaning in fighting for the German fatherland, leading to his nationalist ideology and intense pursuit of a pure Aryan race. His anti-Semitism, having grown exponentially during the war when he found many Jews expressing anti-war sentiment, became of utmost importance to his cause — though no one could expect the lengths to which he would reach for the sake of his Aryan race. For the time being, Adolf Hitler was one of the most vocal supporters of Germany, swaying much of the public over with his promises of hope and strength for the German nation. Hitler was also one of the only public figures to actually bring about the changes he professed, finding ways to bring wealth back to the people and indoctrinating the younger generation through his Hitler Youth program. Thus, Germany appointed Hitler Chancellor in 1933, and merely a year later, the German president, Hindenburg, died and Hitler became both President and Chancellor for the nation.

Finally in a place of power and total control, Hitler quickly made use of his position and militarized his troops in the

Rhineland in 1936, in spite of the fact that such an action directly defied the conditions of the Treaty of Versailles. As Hitler predicted, however, France and Britain did nothing to stop his efforts, giving him the leeway to take things one step further. In 1938, Hitler carried out a forbidden annexation, or Anschluss, of Austria, which again was received with no reaction from any country. Later this lack of response would be termed 'appeasement,' and explained as the thought process by which most nations believed that Hitler's acquisition of unlawful territory would end with the Anschluss. Additionally, no country had any desire to enter into premature warfare following the tragedies of the first war, leading to the hope that Hitler would be appeased with his conquests and war could be avoided. Unfortunately, this hope was not to be realized, though it was not until Hitler went so far as to invade Poland that other countries got involved. In the meantime, Hitler did everything he could to build up the nation's military and prepare to win the war that he, if not everyone else, knew was inevitable.

The German-Soviet Nonaggression Pact

One part of Hitler's preparation involved gauging his nation's strengths and weaknesses, and knowing how to fight in order to win. Thus, Hitler knew that in order to succeed in an invasion against Poland, he would need to ensure that the USSR remained neutral. Germany could take on the Polish with its military, but there was no way Germany could take on both the Polish and the Russians together. In order to take the Soviet Union out of the picture, Hitler met with Josef Stalin on August 23, 1939, to negotiate a non-aggression pact that would ensure peace between Germany and the Soviet Union. Later named the Molotov-Ribbentrop Pact after the two foreign ministers who met to negotiate an agreement, the German-Soviet Nonaggression Pact first and foremost assured that the two nations would refrain from attacking each other for at least ten years, allowing Hitler to freely march on Poland. The pact also included an economic agreement, which stated that Germany would exchange its manufactured goods for the Soviet Union's raw materials, improving economic conditions for both nations. A final, secret, component of the Nonaggression Pact outlined the partition of Poland between the two nations, with Germany receiving one-third and the Soviet Union taking the rest. Some provisional outlining of the rest of Eastern Europe between the two nations was also established, though not in as much definition.

With the pact uniting the two nations and actually helping Germany to invade Poland, Hitler turned his attention to Poland and prepared to make war. While the Anschluss and Germany's invasion of Sudetenland were more justified battles, since both areas were home to Germans who welcomed Hitler's Nazis and felt that Germany was their rightful nation, Hitler's movement into Poland was completely unjustified. Even after Hitler learned of a new and official pact being signed between Great Britain and Poland, ensuring that the British military would intervene should anyone attempt to attack Poland, Hitler still proceeded with his invasion. He also ignored all diplomatic efforts from greater world powers, determined to achieve the greatness he promised, and desperate to fulfill his dreams for an Aryan race. On August 31, 1939, the first members of the German army invaded Poland, and France and Great Britain officially declared war against Germany by 5:00 PM that same day. **World War II had officially begun.**

Meanwhile, the other half of the negotiation, the Soviet Union, was taking advantage of the new nonaggression pact as well and attacked and eventually managed to annex Finland after a four-month war following the pact's passing. The USSR then went on to occupy the Baltic states and seize the Romanian provinces, Bukovina and Bessarabia, by the year 1940. Though the nonaggression pact was supposed to ensure peace between Germany and the Soviet Union, everything changed after World War II officially broke out and nations began taking sides. Since Hitler had always considered the German-Soviet Nonaggression Pact to be a temporary agreement, he chose not to adhere to its policies when it came time for a new tactical maneuver - invade the Soviet Union. With the signing of Directive 21 - code-named Operation Barbarossa - on December 18, 1940, Hitler broke the Nonaggression Pact and officially cut ties with the Soviet Union, since the directive was the first operational order for the invasion of the USSR. The reality of the situation was the Hitler had no intention of maintaining an alliance with the Soviet Union, since the nation's Communist policies and large percentage of Jews directly defiled Hitler's future plans for a pure Aryan race. Therefore, it did not take Hitler long to abandon the provisions of the pact, and on June 22, 1941, German forces invaded the Soviet Union. This was only two years after the Nonaggression Pact had been signed, and proved just how unstable politics could be in a time of war.

Dunkirk

After war was officially declared between Germany, Great Britain, France, and eventually the Soviet Union, many other countries rushed to take sides. Several powerful nations - including Italy, Belgium, Spain, and the U.S. - immediately declared their neutrality, unwilling to become involved in another war so soon after the last one. With many countries understandably hesitant to get involved, Hitler was free to follow his warpath, leaving death and casualties in his wake. Unfortunately, France was one of the first nations on his list, though the defeat of several smaller countries had to come first.

Beginning with the low countries, Germany first targeted the Netherlands and sent its forces in by parachute, targeting key bridges and roadways to aid with mobilizing its own ground troops. By May 13, Queen Wilhelmina and her government left the Netherlands, leaving the Dutch people with no choice but to surrender to the Germans. Incredibly, German troops were invading Belgium at the same time, landing in several key areas of the nation on May 10th. As quickly as the following day the Belgian front was broken, allowing the Germans to push through and force the British and French armies back. Before long, Germany had control of the lower countries, which allowed the nation to focus entirely on conquering France. Though the French army was supported by the British, the Germans were a formidable foe and promised a fearsome battle.

The German invasion of France began with the Germans successfully acquiring the southeastern border of Belgium, which was quickly followed by their access to the Franco-Belgian border, overlooking the Meuse River, on May 12. One particularly important aspect of the German invasion was the nation's early advance through the Ardennes forest, led by General Paul Ludwig von Kleist. This advance allowed the German army to surround and effectively cut off the Allied troops, and though the Allied army attempted several counter-offensive maneuvers, they were never quite successful. Unfortunately, the lack of French troops simply made a counter-attack impossible; the German army was far too strong. With what seemed like a limitless supply of infantry available to relieve their soldiers, the Germans were capable of overwhelming ground that the French did not have definitively covered. Thus, the Germans quickly overwhelmed various areas of France, giving the French troops reason to fear for the survival of their nation. The Germans marching across Aisne on May 15 was particularly terrifying for the French, especially the French commander-in-chief, Maurice Gamelin, because it meant that Paris was in danger. France did not have enough troops to cover Aisne, and they knew that Germany's presence in the area meant that Paris could be compromised. In response, the French Premier, Paul Reynaud, decided it would be safest to move the capital from Paris to Tours, worried that the Germans had advanced far enough to threaten the safety of the capital. When more accurate reports of the front reached Reynaud, however, he realized that moving Paris to Tours was a mistake and the Germans were not making as much progress as they professed. Irritated that France's commander-in-chief had prematurely raised the alarm, Reynaud took advantage of the opportunity to remove Gamelin from his position, sending for General Maxime Weygand from Syria to replace Gamelin as commander-in-chief. Meanwhile, Reynaud informed the people that the decision to move Paris to Tours had been an absurd rumor, hoping to dispel any concerns and maintain whatever morale remained. However, France's situation was still dire, particularly because Gamelin's replacement, Weygand, would not arrive in France until May 19th, leaving the Supreme Command without direction for three full days.

Then, in the next major stage of the German invasion, German troops raced for the English Channel, cutting off Allied forces in Belgium and making their way quickly across France. Advance troops managed to cross Oise on May 17, reaching Amiens two days later and then arriving at Abbeville by the 20th, which effectively managed to block communication between northern and southern France. With Germany's motorized divisions forming a defensive flank along the line of their conquest, it was nearly impossible for the Allies to break through, forcing the Allies to surrender or retreat to the coast. Though John Gort, the commander-in-chief of the British Expeditionary Forces, wanted to retreat by water, he was ordered to take his troops south and fight long range against the Germans. Unfortunately, with his limited resources, Gort could not easily launch an offensive, leaving him with only two divisions in Arras to use for an attack. In spite of their limited resources, the Allies decided to launch the offensive in Arras anyway, beginning on May 21st and managing to do some serious damage on the Germans in the short duration of the offensive. Apparently British light tanks held up well to German antitank weapons, and the resilience of this small operation momentarily shook German High Command. The efforts of the offensive at Arras, however, were not enough to do any long-lasting damage. Before long, the Allied forces in the north were rushing to the English Channel to retreat, though whether or not they would make it to the coast before the Germans arrived was another question.

After the Belgians sued for armistice on May 27th, Weygand made one last attempt to salvage the situation in France and sent troops to fill the crack that the Germans broke through the Allied defensive line, but it was too late. The German army could not be stopped. Unfortunately, Weygand's efforts were also partly thwarted by his outdated tactics and inability to keep up with the new terms and technology of the Second World War. This led many soldiers to believe that Weygand was ill-prepared to lead in the second war, a belief that was never really remedied over the course of the war.

Even before Belgium's fall and Weygand's final attempt to hold the line, the British prepared to launch Operation Dynamo, a final operation which would evacuate the British Expeditionary Forces and other Allied troops by sea from Dunkirk. Both the Royal Air Force and the Royal Navy were assigned to cover the fleeing troops and keep the Germans at bay, but in spite of the assistance, most people assumed that the operation would be only 25% successful at best. Bertram Ramsay had overall command of the operation, and William Tennant had tactical oversight. When Tennant arrived in Dunkirk on May 27 to assess the situation, however, he was met with distress. The Luftwaffe had managed to destroy all of the port's facilities, leaving the retreating soldiers with minimal resources for evacuation. Thus, Tennant quickly called upon all manner of ships or boats available to help, taking everything from the British Navy's destroyers and battleships to civilian yachts and fishing boats. Tennant also determined that using Dunkirk's eastern breakwater for picking up the troops would be less time consuming than having the ships retrieve troops from the beach, and this effort indeed saved a considerable amount of time during the evacuation. Of the 330,000 troops evacuated during Operation Dynamo, 200,000 used the eastern breakwater to board the ships, while the rest had to be picked up from the beach.

Beginning on May 26, the evacuation of the Allied troops from Dunkirk was finally complete on June 4th, with Tennant radioing in the initial completion of the evacuation on June 2nd. After Tennant radioed Ramsay at the Doer post for Operation Dynamo, saying the BEF had officially been evacuated, the final commanders conducted a last roundup for any straggling soldiers and officially declared the evacuation complete on June 4th. Overall, 198,000 BEF troops and 140,000 Allied troops, mostly French soldiers, were evacuated by the end of Operation Dynamo. Since the British imperial staff had expected less than 25% of the troops in France to be successfully evacuated from Dunkirk, the resulting 330,000 rescued troops was a significant victory for Britain and far exceeded everyone's expectations for Operation Dynamo.

Ironically, the primary person who brought about the miracle of Dunkirk was Hitler himself, who called his troops back the moment they were set to invade Dunkirk. There are several reasons cited for this unusual decision, starting with Hitler's overestimation of the British fight at Arres, which meant that he relocated an unnecessary amount of troops to the Arres front when the Allied forces there managed to hold up as well as they did. Another reason cited was voiced by one of Hitler's highest generals, General Gerd von Rundstedt, who reminded Hitler that Germany needed to conserve armored divisions for the next stage of battle, making a pursuit of fleeing soldiers an unnecessary waste for the Germans. Additionally, the German air force commander insisted that he could handle the troops at Dunkirk with his squadron alone, allowing Germany's ground troops to be deployed elsewhere. Hitler also had personal experience with the marshy lands of the north, and he feared that sending a ground force into Dunkirk would result in a giant mess of stuck tanks and lost resources. Lastly, some of Hitler's closest generals claimed that Hitler intentionally allowed the Allied troops to escape at Dunkirk, believing that the British would only make peace with Germany in the end if they were not forced to disgracefully surrender. Regardless of the reason, Hitler made it possible for the Allied troops at Dunkirk to retreat to England almost without any interference from the Germans. It was a significant win for the Allies.

In spite of the miracle of Dunkirk, however, the reality of the situation could not be ignored; Dunkirk was still a retreat and still represented significant defeat for the British. While many troops were saved, all of their weapons and supplies had to be left behind on the beaches, leaving the soldiers with little to use in later battles. Additionally, 50,000 troops were captured or killed leading up to the evacuation, and most of those captured would remain in German prisoner of war camps until the war officially ended several years later.

The Battle of Britain

Shortly after Germany defeated France in June of 1940 and the miracle of Dunkirk had taken place, Hitler targeted southern England with a major air campaign that he hoped would lower the nation's defenses. Though he originally assumed that the British would want to make a peace settlement with Germany once the French were defeated, Hitler soon discovered that the British were determined to keep fighting, making it necessary for him to target the homeland if he hoped to get them to surrender. Thus, Hitler put his air campaign in motion, intending to secure the air over southern England before conducting an amphibious invasion to overwhelm the nation's coast. Titled Operation Sealion, the amphibious invasion would hopefully result in British surrender, ending Germany's war with Britain and allowing the Germans to focus all of their attention on the Soviet Union. But in order for any of that to happen, Hitler had to take out the British Royal Air Force first, and that was no small feat.

The British Royal Air Force, or the RAF, was developed in 1918 as an independent branch of the British air force. Though the branch started out small and took it's time growing, the RAF eventually boomed in the 1930s, which was mainly in response to the development of Nazi Germany. Then, in 1936, RAF Fighter Command Leadership fell to Air Marshal Sir Hugh Dowding, after whom the Dowding System was named. The Dowding System, a new system for tactical planning, brought ground defense, technology, and fighter aircraft into a unified system that was previously unparalleled in war. The Dowding

System was especially valuable for allowing massive amounts of information to be processed in a short period of time, enabling Fighter Command to fully utilize every last one of its valuable and relatively limited resources. Additionally, the British Royal Air Force boasted of a seamless defense system, which was organized to ensure the best response time possible. First, the defense was split into four geographical areas called "groups," with each group divided into sectors with one main airfield per sector. Then, the airfield's sector station, equipped with an operations room, directed fighters in combat and gave them constantly updated information on the frontlines. Finally, the British had a considerable technological weapon at their disposal; the radar. Radar, or Radio Direction Finding, allowed the British to track the movements of the Luftwaffe, eliminating the element of surprise for the Germans' attacks. With the radar patching directly to the Observer Corps, any valuable information on incoming raids was then passed to the Filter Room at Bentley Priority's Fighter Command Headquarters. Once the information about the raid was processed, it was distributed to the relevant group's headquarters before being sent on to the sector stations that directly scrambled fighters into action. From there, each sector station received information from radio as it became available, allowing the pilots to be radioed constant updates as events in the battle unfolded. These advances, combined with the fact that the British were hosts to two of the best fighter airplanes in the world; the Hawker Hurricane, and the Submarine Spitfire; made the RAF very difficult to beat. In spite of the powerful aspect of the RAF, however, the German Luftwaffe made for a considerable enemy. Though Germany was banned from building an air force, Hitler disregarded that policy when he came into office and quickly made the Luftwaffe the largest and most formidable air force in the world. Even after the battle with France, the Germans managed to salvage their

Luftwaffe and appeared to be coming at Britain stronger than ever. Thus, the Battle of Britain was almost entirely a test of strength between the Luftwaffe and the RAF, and the best squadron would definitely win.

The Battle of Britain was fought between July and October of 1940, with Germany beginning the offensive by targeting coastal targets and British shipping operations in the English Channel. From there, the Luftwaffe planned to move inland, focusing on airfields and communication centers. The first surprise airborne raid, launched by the Germans on July 10th, 1940, targeted a British shipping convoy on the English Channel. Though the British suffered some severe damage under the Luftwaffe, the Fighter Command did not budge and offered stiff resistance to the Germans, forcing them to intensify their attack. By the last week of August and the first week of September, the Germans were directly targeting the Fighter Command, making those few weeks a critical part of the battle with Britain. Miraculously the British managed to salvage most of their airfields and keep them operational, even with the Luftwaffe wreaking considerable havoc. Unfortunately, August 31st witnessed the worst day of casualties for the Fighter Command, and the Luftwaffe sincerely believed that they were winning and that Fighter Command was finished. Yet again, the British proved they were not to be underestimated, and the Fighter Command, though shaken, was not broken. The RAF soldiered on and war continued, but with every passing day, extreme levels of exhaustion and lack of preparation increased for both nations. In many cases, pilots were flying several missions a day without respite, or were even fighting after as little as nine hours' worth of training. There would have to be a shift in the battle soon as neither side was equipped to fight for much longer.

Then, on the 7th of September, the Luftwaffe made a critical mistake by shifting their attacks from RAF fields and communication zones to the city of London. Though the Luftwaffe caused serious damage in London, the momentary respite from their battle with the RAF gave the fighters time to recover and come back to Great Britain's defense. It was this mistake that may have cost Germany the war. When the Luftwaffe attacked again on September 15, the British fought back and managed to inflict serious damage on the Germans; damage from which they could not recover. All of a sudden, it was becoming imminently clear that Germany was not going to win the battle against Britain, and Hitler postponed Operation Sealion indefinitely. Operation Sealion would never be addressed again.

Though the Royal Air Force was only comprised of 3,000 men - of whom Churchill said, "never in the field of human conflict was so much owed by so many to so few"- they were a powerful, international few with members from all over the world. And the few were not alone; they had the overwhelming support of the ground crew, factory workers, Observer Corps, anti-aircraft gunners, and searchlight operations working to make sure that everything went as smoothly as possible. In addition, the Women's Auxiliary Air Force (WAAF) and the 1.5 million men who joined the Local Defence Volunteers aided the cause of the RAF, turning 'the few' into 'the many.' These individuals' collective efforts were truly what saved the day and won the battle against Germany.

With the Luftwaffe having sustained severe damage from the battle that even surpassed the damage the British received, the Germans were forced to cut back their invasion and change tactics. In spite of its previous number and force, the Luftwaffe was devastatingly crippled, and it would take an invaluable amount of time to return the air force to its previous strength. By the conclusion of the battle, the Germans lost over 1,700 planes; nearly twice as many as the British lost in combat. Overall, this battle proved to be one of Britain's most significant victories in WWII, both for the damage it caused the Luftwaffe, and for the confidence and fighting spirit it gave to all of Great Britain. Even though Germany's blitzkrieg over Britain did not end until May of 1941 and killed over 40,000 people in the process, Hitler turned his attention briefly to the Soviet Union. For the moment, Britain had won.

Pearl Harbor

Later in 1941, a newly threatening battle was taking place on the opposite side of the world from the war in Europe, with the U.S. and Japan preparing for a significant battle in the Pacific Ocean Theater. Though the U.S. had no reason to suspect it, the Japanese were making their way to Pearl Harbor, the home base for much of the U.S.'s resources in the Pacific. With most of the United States' battleships in port and planes clustered on the airfields, Pearl Harbor made for a risky but ideal target for the Japanese, especially if they could incorporate the element of surprise.

Having long studied the U.S.'s movements and patterns in the Pacific, the Japanese quickly took note of the fact that the U.S. Navy returned to Pearl Harbor every weekend for respite. With the battleships and airplanes as sitting ducks for an air offensive, this made Pearl Harbor the ideal candidate for Japan's next target. However, Pearl Harbor was a very dangerous mission for the same reason it was the perfect target; should the Americans learn of Japan's plan, they could be armored and readily awaiting the arrival of the Japanese, inflicting serious damage before the Japanese could even take aim. Thus, the leaders of the attack on Pearl Harbor insisted on developing detailed backup attacks, determined to only retreat without a fight if they were discovered prematurely. The commanders of the attack on Pearl Harbor, Commanders Mitsuo Fuchida and Minoru Genda, were both young aviators who believed that aviation could determine the course of war, unlike the older generation of Japanese who believed that war depended primarily on battleships. With Vice-Admiral Chuichi Nagumo, an older Japanese commander, in charge of carrying out Fuchida and Genda's plans, Pearl Harbor represented the perfect target for all generations and allowed for the Japanese to both sink battleships and ground airplanes. The hope with the attack on Pearl Harbor was to neutralize the U.S.'s power in the Pacific Basin for at least six months, allowing Japan the opportunity to occupy the East Asian and West Pacific regions in the U.S.'s absence. Then, with Japan in full control of the Pacific Basin, the U.S. and the other Allies would be forced to negotiate a settlement, giving Imperialist Japan the victory. Of course, that was only if everything with the attack on Pearl Harbor went smoothly, and that was no guarantee.

Commanders Fuchida and Genda's plan of attack began by sending a six carrier task force all the way from Japan through the empty sea between Hawaii and the Aleutian Islands. Then, once the carrier force was in place, floater planes would be sent out to observe the Americans' activities at Pearl Harbor and Lahaina Roads in order to determine which target would reap the most benefits for the Japanese. Once this information was gathered and delivered back to the carriers, the offensive would commence, which ultimately meant that timing was everything if the attack was to go smoothly. Additionally, the Japanese bombers were also equipped with specially adapted 16 inch naval shells, which were designed to pierce the armored decks of the U.S. battleships in port. The hope was that the naval shells would also detonate the powder magazines in the battleships, blowing the ships to pieces and making salvage impossible. Thus, even if the Japanese targeted Pearl Harbor, which had shallow ports that typically allowed for ships to be salvaged, the detonation of the ships' powder magazines would blow them apart and make salvaging entirely useless. Collectively, all of these plans revealed just how meticulous the

Japanese were in constructing their attack, leaving no detail left to chance. If they were going to be totally successful, they would need to operate on the element of surprise, and that meant planning for every possible setback along the way.

Though no one saw the attack at Pearl Harbor coming, everyone anticipated war in the Pacific by November 25th. The only question was, where? While the rest of the world expected war to break out in Indochina, the Dutch East Indies, and the Philippines, the Japanese knew that the next stage for battle was, in fact, Oahu, though the Japanese cleverly deployed 200 naval vessels into the southeast as a preamble to war, making for the perfect diversion. With political negotiations breaking down and war becoming more inevitable with every passing day, all major American commands in the Pacific received warnings that they should be prepared to fight. In spite of these warnings, however, only one person suspected that Pearl Harbor would be the target of the next Japanese attack.

When Admiral Husband Kimmel met with other generals and commanders in Oahu on November 27, the plan was to move aircraft from Pearl Harbor to Wake and Midway Islands in order to build up defenses there. Lieutenant James Mollison, however, was against the idea, saying that Japan had the capability of attacking Oahu and the aircraft should stay in case Oahu needed defending. Captain Horatio McMorris replied that while the Japanese could, hypothetically, attack Oahu, they had no motivation to do so. Despite McMorris' avid reassurances that Oahu was safe, Admiral Kimmel did not feel so confident, and he chose to leave the aircraft where they were grounded in Pearl Harbor. Of course, Kimmel's decision to keep the aircraft at Oahu ultimately resulted in more wreckage and total success for Japan's attack, though Kimmel could never have predicted that result. Nothing else about protecting

Pearl Harbor was mentioned following the meeting, even though several Japanese carrier ships were unaccounted for and the U.S. was still not sure where the Japanese would choose to attack. Unfortunately, Intelligence Bureaus were busy tracking the Japanese Navy in the south and did not have time to worry about two missing carrier groups, especially since those two carrier groups had actually been missing as many as twelve times during the war; one more time was no cause for concern. Additionally, the Intelligence Bureaus were struggling with a recent set of newly developed callsigns, which made their work time-consuming and meant they did not have time to investigate concerns for an unlikely attack at Oahu. Pearl Harbor was supposed to be a reliable supply for armies all over the Pacific, never the target for an attack or the cause of havoc and chaos. By the end of the year, however, Pearl Harbor would be both, leaving many military stations without supplies and putting a halt to most military operations in the Pacific.

Meanwhile, Japanese Vice-Admiral Chuichi Nagumo was headed for Hawaii with his strike fleet and Commanders Fuchida and Genda at his side. In spite of the commanders' assurance that attacking on both fronts was necessary, Nagumo was still worried about the offensive. He was certain that the Americans would anticipate the Japanese attack at Pearl Harbor, resulting in heavy losses for Japan's air fleet. Regardless of Nagumo's concerns, however, six of Japan's biggest aircraft carriers were steaming toward Oahu, planning to station themselves a mere 200 miles away from the Americans in the Pacific Ocean. The metaphorical cream-of-the-Japanese-aviation-crop was ready for battle, and even Nagumo knew that attacking Pearl Harbor was the next big step for Imperialist Japan. If Japan truly hoped to advance in the war and make considerable progress, attacking Pearl Harbor was a necessary choice, risk or not.

On December 3rd, a warning was sent to Kimmel's Port Harbor Command, saying "...categoric and urgent instructions were sent yesterday to Japanese diplomatic and consular posts at Hong Kong, Singapore, Batavia, Manila, Washington and London to destroy most of their codes and ciphers at once and to burn all other important confidential and secret documents." Still, Pearl Harbor did not prepare for war, and American Vice Admiral William "Bull" Halsey took the aircraft carrier *Enterprise* out to Wake with a fleet of battleships, which were sent out to their exercise area while the *Enterprise* headed west with a heavy escort of cruisers and destroyers. Once it reached open seas, the *Enterprise* issued Battle Order Number One - "The *Enterprise* is now operating under war conditions . . ." - and Halsey believed that by the time his carrier returned to Pearl Harbor, Japan and the Allies would be at war. As it turned out, he was right. Little did he know, the warfront would be much closer to home than he anticipated.

Meanwhile, Kimmel had the U.S. battleships resting safely at the port in Pearl Harbor, knowing that there they could be protected from enemy air attack should any unexpected offensive occur. He also had the aircraft neatly lined up for observation, unfortunately making for a very easy target once the Japanese arrived. Though Kimmel's plans were strategic had the base anticipated Japan's arrival, their lack of preparation and total surprise made them sitting ducks when Japan did eventually attack Pearl Harbor. Additionally, the U.S. made the unfortunate decision to take the weekend of December 7th off, in spite of all the warnings and alerts that the Japanese would attack in the Pacific soon. Thus, all of Pearl Harbor was asleep when the Japanese awoke the morning of their offensive. As the leader of the torpedo bombers, Lt. Commander Shigeharu Murata, told Commander Fuchida, "The Honolulu radio plays soft music . . . everything is fine."

The first planes to attack were Itaya's fighters, who targeted Kaneohe Naval Air Station seven minutes before the attack reached Pearl Harbor. Then, by 0615 the morning of December 7th, 1941, the first wave of the Japanese offensive, 183 aircraft in total, was launched in a record 15 minutes. With their meticulous planning and grueling labor already paying off, the Japanese army began the massive attack against Pearl Harbor that would have devastating results, effectively pitting Imperial Japan against the rest of the world. Despite their careful planning, however, Fuchida's command for first positions resulted in near chaos, with both dive bombers and torpedo bombers assuming their first positions in the confusion of having two plans for initial attack. Though Fuchida was frustrated and worried that his meticulous planning was unravelling right before his eyes, he quickly realized how completely unaware the Americans really were, making the careful efforts of the Japanese almost entirely unnecessary. With no alert sounded, even after unidentified planes were sighted by radar, the Japanese had all the time in the world to launch their offensive and ensure they made use of all of their resources. This meant that the Japanese planes swept over their targets a few times before launching their weapons, which resulted in their targets being hit every time and that the Japanese offensive appeared to be larger than it actually was. It also meant that the Americans did have some time to recover and respond. Though the Japanese were shocked by how quickly the Americans responded after being a state of total repose, their efforts would still not be enough.

Japan's first target in the offensive was Wheeler Field, the U.S. Army base on Oahu, which was followed by the U.S. Army's air field, Hickam Field, and finally, the U.S. Navy field based on Ford Island. Thankfully, the U.S.'s carriers were not stationed at Pearl Harbor, which minimized some of the damage, but there were more than enough targets for the Japanese to hit. Following the initial wave of the attack, the Nakajima "Kate" torpedo bombers under Murata caused the worst destruction of the day, inflicting serious damage on the unprotected ships on Battleship Row. One of the battleships in port, the *Nevada*, managed to survive with damage from only one torpedo. This ship, the only one to have its machine guns manned, provided a reasonable defense for itself and prevented Japanese airplanes from getting too close, though, unfortunately, most of the other battleships were not so lucky. Then, in another fly-by, the Japanese bomber planes began dropping their loads on the ships, destroying what the torpedoes did not already hit. Of all the deaths suffered by the Americans in the attack, half of them were caused by the destruction of the *Arizona*, which exploded when its powder magazines were hit by a well-timed bomb. As the *Arizona* detonated in a devastating explosion, many of the crew died and the ship split in two, finally coming to rest at the bottom of the harbor. Then, when the *Arizona*'s hull finally settled, the ship broke the water line leading to Ford Island, crippling firefighting efforts and further frustrating the Americans' attempts at defense. Before long, the *Arizona* was also pouring oil into the water, causing more fires and forcing the Americans to use the *Tennessee*'s fire hoses to keep the situation in check. With the entirety of their forces concentrated on salvaging as much as possible, the Americans had no time to prepare for a counter-offensive. The best they could do was hold down the fort and keep the fires at bay, waiting for the end to come.

Once the Japanese torpedo and high-level bombers had completed their missions, dive bombers and fighters swooped in to hit their own assigned target areas, perfectly executing the final stage of their first attack before retreating. The momentary peace at Pearl Harbor was not to last long, however, because before long a second wave of fighters hit, with 167 new aircraft sent in for renewed attack. It was during this second part of the fight that the *Nevada* attempted to escape, making a break for the open sea. Before the *Nevada* could get very far, however, the Japanese bombed her as well, doing everything they could to sink the ship in the hopes that it would paralyze the Americans for months. Though the *Nevada* did not make it to open sea, it did not sink entirely, and was gently grounded for later salvaging. Additionally, the *Pennsylvania* eventually managed to send up considerable flak, limiting the damage done by the Japanese on that ship. As for the other ships, many of them did not fare so well. That included the *Shaw*, whose front end disintegrated when fires on board finally reached the forward magazines in the front end of the ship. This ship's demise became one of the most dramatic and most photographed event of the day. Thankfully, by 0930 the attacks had given way to sporadic strafing, and the worst of the attack on Pearl Harbor was over, though it wasn't until 0945 that the last of the strafing planes left for their rendezvous point northwest of Oahu.

While the Americans awaited the return of the Japanese, doing the best they could to prepare for the invasion that was inevitable, the Japanese regrouped and awaited commands. Though Fuchida was thrilled with Japan's success and believed that another attack was necessary in order to seal the fate of the U.S., Nagumo decided to call off a follow-up attack or invasion, believing that the Japanese had been lucky and should quit while they were ahead. Though they originally planned on hunting down the U.S.'s carriers, Nagumo had no intention of tempting fate and risking another operation. Though Fuchida was incensed by this decision, believing that the Japanese had not taken full advantage of the risk they took when they attacked Pearl Harbor, there was nothing to be done. The Japanese retreated, and the Americans were left to salvage the mess as best they could. By the end of the attack on Pearl Harbor, 2,403 Americans were killed, and the U.S. Pacific Fleet was officially in ruins.

In spite of the devastation of Pearl Harbor, later speculation of the attack revealed that in reality, the Japanese were simply delaying the inevitable; the Americans were a war machine that could not be stopped. Considering the amount of damage that the Japanese could have inflicted on the Americans, the destruction of Pearl Harbor was considerably salvageable and would actually facilitate repairs. Of the Americans' battleships at port, only two of them were beyond saving, and then four of them were back at sea within two weeks of the attack. The reality of the situation was that Japan's attack was little more than a kick to the hornet's nest, which mostly just angered the U.S. and was more effective at mobilizing troops than any other tactic they had attempted. Therefore, despite the success of the Japanese attack at Pearl Harbor, the risk of the attack and its resulting effects likely outweighed its benefits. Regardless, the losses at Pearl Harbor were great for the U.S., and the memory of those who lost their lives in the attack will always be remembered. As President Franklin D. Roosevelt said, December 7th, 1941 was a "day that would live in infamy."

The Destruction of Cologne

As the Allies gained power in the war and tides began to shift in their favor. They began developing new tactical fighting plans and techniques to push them ahead of the Axis powers once and for all. In one of the war's greatest tactical maneuvers, Sir Arthur Harris led a 1,000 bomber raid over the German city of Cologne, wreaking havoc and destruction in ways previously not thought possible. When Sir Arthur Harris first approached Winston Churchill and Sir Charles Portal with his idea to successively bomb a German city with 1,000 bombers, the leaders were incredulous. Admittedly, Harris had plans for ensuring perfect unity among his bombers to avoid collisions and collateral damage, but successfully completing a mission of that size seemed impossible. However, Churchill and Portal eventually approved of Harris' idea, allowing him to go forward with the plan, so long as he could amass enough trained pilots and planes to pull off the offensive. Of course, accomplishing that feat would prove to be more of a challenge.

With his plan approved, Harris began searching for the resources he needed to successfully accomplish a full 1,000 bomber offensive. Unfortunately, Harris only ever worked with 400 planes, meaning that he would need to salvage a considerable number of aircraft from other areas of the British Air Force. Harris began by requesting planes from Bomber Command and Flying Training Command, which resulted in him acquiring 300 aircraft total. While Sir Philip Joubert of Coastal Command immediately provided 250 bombers, many of which had served in squadrons for Bomber Command, the leaders at Flying Training Command offered only 50 aircraft, and most of those planes were later found to be insufficiently equipped for night bombing. Unfortunately, only four Wellingtons were able to be culled from this source in the end, leaving Harris with far too few aircraft to achieve the 1,000 bombers he needed to succeed.

While Harris continued searching for more bombers to use, he began further detailing plans for the tactical aspect of the bombing. Eventually, the tactics Harris developed would become the basis for standard Bomber Command operations, with some elements remaining in use through the rest of the war. Harris' main invention, the bomber stream, transformed the speed and efficiency of bomber tactics, allowing for a much more rapid attack than ever before. In the bomber stream, aircraft flew along a set route at the exact same speed to and from the target, with each plane allotted a height band and time slot in the hopes of minimizing collisions. Using the bomber stream not only meant increased efficiency and lessened collateral damage, it also meant that the aircraft would pass through fewer German radar night-fighter boxes. This would decrease the amount of possible interceptions for the bombers and would allow them to pass through the belt of boxes more quickly, so long as the raid was kept as short and succinct as possible. When it came to conducting a more rapid bomber raid, then, Harris was nothing if not insanely ambitious. Whereas most bomber raids for about 100 aircraft took around four hours and the record time was set at two hours for 234 aircraft at Lubeck, Harris wanted to achieve his 1,000 bomber raid in a mere 90 minutes. Though this goal was incredibly dangerous and encouraged far more midair collisions, Harris determined that the minimal time was necessary if all of his objectives were to be met. After all, Harris' aim for the 1,000 bombing raid was to have his aircraft passed through the night-fighter boxes quickly, ensuring that they could then overtake the defensive flak at the target and cause enough fires from their high concentration of bombs that the fire department would be overwhelmed and unable to save the entire city from going up in flames. With these goals in mind, Harris was determined to do whatever it took to achieve them. Unfortunately, not everyone was on his side.

Having discovered that 250 bombers had been given to Harris for the raid, the Admiralty in charge of Coastal Command suddenly withdrew the Coastal Command's donation, refusing to allow their aircraft to fly as a part of Harris' mission. Unfortunately, Britain's Royal Air Force and Royal Navy were struggling for control of maritime air power at the time, leading to increased hostilities and disrupted communication between both branches. Once the Admiralty recognized that aiding Bomber Command meant crippling their own prospects for building a force to combat the German U-boat, they refused to provide assistance for Harris' mission. Though Harris himself had nothing to do with the struggle for power, the situation remained the same; the Admiralty would not willingly help Bomber Command claim a serious victory, ensuring them maritime air power, if they could help it. Thus, Harris was down by 250 aircraft and had limited options if he wanted the 1,000 bomber raid to succeed. He would have to become resourceful.

In what would later be considered a massive public relations exercise, Harris and the Bomber Command redoubled their efforts, ensuring that every spare aircraft in the squadron was retrieved to fulfill the 1,000 bomber need. Though this effort was successful, it did require that some of Bomber Command's unprepared pilots fly in the raid. In the end, Harris did everything he could to ensure that each training crew had at least one experienced pilot on board, but there were still 49 aircraft out of the 208 provided by 91 Group that would take off with pilots-in-training.

Finally Harris' hard work paid off, and he managed to acquire 1,047 planes for his operation, with only four of those planes supplied by Training Command and the rest coming from Bomber Command. Since the raid was two and a half times greater than any single night's effort by Bomber Command, Harris was prepared to lose 100 planes in the mission, a number which, though appalling, was really somewhat reasonable given the unprecedented size and timing of the raid. Additionally, Harris managed to acquire several other planes to fly alongside his bombers and conduct Intruder raids on the night-fighter airfields near the bomber stream, providing more protection for the bombers and running interference for any German efforts. With everything in place at last, final orders were ready on the 26th of May, 1942, with a full moon approaching. The only question that remained was which city to target.

Harris' first choice target was Hamburg, the second largest city in Germany and a port for building German U-boats, making it a devastating target for his massive raid. Unfortunately, weather over Hamburg proved to be a bit difficult, and though Harris waited as long as he could, conditions never improved over the city. Finally, by the 30th of May, Harris caved and sent out orders to commence with the operation for his second choice of target: the third-largest city in Germany, Cologne. The bomber raid was a go and finally commenced on the clear, moonlit evening of May 30th.

With bombers taking off at 22.30 from 53 bases across Britain, crews were told to follow the River Rhine once they reached

Western Europe, using it as a guide to lead them straight to Cologne. Since the first bombers to arrive had to lead the way to Cologne, they were the most modern aircraft in the raid and were equipped with GEE navigational equipment. Once they arrived, these aircraft had fifteen minutes alone with the city, giving them time to target the Neumarkt in the city's old town and initiate enough fires to create a sort of beacon for other planes to follow. Then, the other bombers coming in were assigned targets one mile north or south of the Neumarkt, which ensured that each bomber could easily find its target and spread fires throughout the city. Overall, the 1,000 bombers dropped a total tonnage of 1,455 bombs, with two-thirds of them being incendiaries. The result was 2,500 fires started in Cologne, and between 469 and 486 deaths, particularly since this was the 105th time in the war that air raid sirens went off in Cologne, which meant that many individuals doubted the validity of the sirens and refused to seek shelter. By the time the people of Cologne realized that the bomb threat was real, bombs were already dropping from the sky and there was nothing to be done. Overall, the attack destroyed 600 acres (300 acres of the city center), and 13,000 homes, damaged 6,000 other homes, left 45,000 people homeless, and resulted in over 5,000 casualties. Additionally, industrial life around the city was frozen for a week, and it took the city about six months to fully recover and return to industry. Later, it was revealed that the intensity of the attack was so great that the final run of bombers could see the glow of the flames from 100 miles away, with smoke from the fires rising to as high as 15,000 feet. For a week following the attack, the immense density of the smoke over Cologne actually made it difficult for the RAF to acquire any decent reconnaissance photos of the city. Harris had accomplished his incredible feat, and Cologne was left to suffer the consequences of his success.

Meanwhile, Harris' bombers fared far better than the city of Cologne, with only four bombers lost in collisions over the city and 35 lost to the efforts of German night-fighters. Miraculously, this was only 4% of the bombers involved in the raid, and less than half the amount that Bomber Command could afford to lose. For an initial attempt at a tricky new maneuver, such results were not bad at all. In fact, the success of the first raid led to Harris attempting another 1,000 bomber raid at Essen, since he had hoped that his 1,000 bomber strategy would be used more than once in the war. Unfortunately, the second raid was not nearly as successful as the first, and none of the raids following Essen made it back up to the 1,000 mark, nor lived up to the initial offensive at Cologne. In spite of the lesser success of the later raids, massive numbers of bombers were still called upon from time to time, but never to the extent to which Harris had hoped. In spite of that, the raid certainly made its mark on history and resulted in new, successful tactics for raids to come. Progressively, the tactics used in the 1,000 bomber raid would allow for 700 or 800 aircraft to participate in raids, passing over a city in less than twenty minutes. The British front line was also pushed for the rest of the summer, bombers targeting German cities when the weather was clear and retreating to coastal targets when it was not. Overall, the success of the raid increased publicity for the Bomber Command and greatly boosted morale for the British, and the ambitious 'Bomber' Harris remained in the public eye for the rest of his life.

The Battle of Midway

Shortly after the 1,000 bomber raid at Cologne, another battle between the U.S. and Japan broke out in the Pacific Theater, beginning June 3rd, 1942 and ending on the 6th. In one of the largest naval battles of World War II, the United States damaged Japan's carrier strength and eliminated many of the nation's best-trained naval pilots. Alongside the Battle of Guadalcanal, the Battle of Midway effectively put an end to further invasion of the Japanese in the Pacific. The Battle of Midway was also fought almost entirely with aircraft, with the battleships and carrier fleets receiving most of the damage.

Following May 1942, the indecisive Battle of the Coral Sea left Japan struggling, though the Japanese eventually decided that it was necessary for them to continue with plans to seize Midway Island and bases in the Aleutians if they wanted to have a chance at taking the Pacific Theater once and for all. Japan also wanted to have a naval showdown with the U.S. Pacific fleet, since the Japanese fleet was numerically bigger and had become a considerable force on the Pacific front. Thus, the Japanese began making plans to seize Midway Island, which included a feint to Alaska by a smaller Japanese fleet in the hopes of drawing the American carrier fleet away from Midway and into a trap. Overall, the Japanese wanted revenge for the U.S.'s Tokyo Air Raid, which bombed Japan's home islands two months earlier. They also wanted to close the gap in their Eastern defensive perimeter, which was disrupted by the U.S.'s control of Midway, and they hoped to finish off the U.S. Pacific Fleet entirely, perhaps even invading and taking

Hawaii along the way. If these goals could be met, the Japanese Navy would essentially have control of the Pacific and would have direct access to the U.S. West Coast, which would be entirely defenseless since the rest of the U.S. Navy was deployed halfway around the world in the North Atlantic. In fact, arguments regarding Japan's actual plans following its destruction of the U.S. Pacific Fleet vary, with some saying that the Japanese only wanted regional conquest, not conquest of North America, and would have left the U.S. alone, whereas others argue that either attack or the threat of attack on the U.S. West Coast would have been enough to divert American military assets away from Europe and toward their homeland. This diversion would, therefore, lengthen the war in the European Theater, giving Japan more time to resurrect the Axis powers and even win the war. Most importantly, however, Japan needed a win, and Midway was the perfect place to start. Though Midway was not, in and of itself, all that important in Japan's overall war plans - after all, Japan was hoping to expand their newly conquered southeastern Pacific territory through the acquisition of the Samoan Islands, Fiji and Australia - it was the last U.S. base that remained closest to Japan, and would be heavily guarded by the Americans. Thus, conquering and acquiring Midway would be a considerable victory for Japan, and would give the nation the base they needed to create an unbreakable front.

On June 3rd, Admiral Yamamoto Isoroku sent the majority of the Japanese Naval fleet toward Midway, instructing the initial fleet's four heavy and three light aircraft carriers to invade Midway and destroy the U.S. Naval fleet along the way. Yamamoto's complicated plans for the offensive included trailing the initial carrier fleet with his main naval force, which would target any of the U.S. Navy that tried to come to Midway's defense. For the most part, the increased complication of Japan's plans for invasion was a direct result of the recent Tokyo Air Raid by U.S. Army B-25s, which proved that the Japanese homeland was not immune from an attack by the Americans. Thus, the Japanese did everything they could to cover their plans with secrecy and confusion, preventing the U.S. from discovering their tactics prematurely. Unfortunately, Japan's carefully concealed and articulated plans were all for naught, U.S. Intelligence broke the Japanese naval codes and, before long, knew everything about their plans.

Though U.S. Intelligence had divined that the Japan intended to attack and was able to send for three heavy aircraft carriers from the U.S. Pacific Fleet, they had yet to determine the location of the target. All Intelligence knew was that the codename for the target was AF, and until they could determine the location of the intended target, their information on Japan's tactical plan was useless. Thankfully, a young officer at Station Hypo, Jasper Holmes, suggested that the base commander at Midway send a radio message to Pearl Harbor, saying in plain English that there was an emergency at the base and they were running low on drinking water. As Holmes had predicted, a JN-25 message sent shortly thereafter stated that AF was having water problems, and that the imminent attack plans should accommodate to those restrictions accordingly. Thus, AF meant Midway, and the U.S. could easily make tactical plans for their counterattack.

With their newly acquired knowledge of Japan's attack, the U.S. began the backbreaking labor of transforming the carrier *Yorktown* in a mere 72 hours from a barely-operational wreck into a working aircraft carrier. The presence of *Yorktown* in the Battle of Midway undoubtedly altered the course of the entire fight, considering the fact that the Japanese had assumed the United States would only be able to send the *Enterprise* and the *Hornet* under Admiral Spruance to meet the Imperial Fleet's four best aircraft carriers; *Soryu, Hiryu, Akagi,* and *Kaga*. Had the Japanese any idea that the *Yorktown* would be added to the U.S. Naval defense, then perhaps they would have been better prepared. As it was, however, the Japanese carriers, having reached their destination about 350 miles northeast of Midway, waited in advance for Yamamoto's armada. War was coming, whether they were ready for it or not.

When the battle officially began on June 3rd, 1942, U.S. bombers from Midway Island attacked the Japanese invasion force, which was located about 220 miles southwest of where the U.S. fleet was stationed. The next morning, Japanese striker planes bombed Midway, while their aircraft carriers did everything they could to escape damage from the U.S. planes that had been based on Hawaii and Midway. Having land-based plans proved to be a huge advantage for the U.S., since they could supply around 115 land-based planes while the Japanese did not have any. Following their attack, the Japanese bombers returned to their aircraft carriers, where Admiral Chuichi Nagumo decided to replenish their bomb supply in preparation for a second offensive against Midway. It was while the planes were being serviced that the Japanese detected U.S. ships nearby, which Nagumo eventually decided would be a better target than Midway. He issued the command for the planes' bombs to be exchanged with a more appropriate arms load, leaving the carriers dangerously vulnerable with scores of bombs, torpedoes, and fuel hoses covering their decks. That, of course, was when the Americans arrived. Before the Japanese could get their aircraft back into the sky, the U.S. launched their attack from the carriers *Enterprise* and *Hornet* under the command of Admiral Spruance. Though the

Japanese managed to shoot down nearly all of the U.S.'s TBD Devastator torpedo bombers and every plane of the *Hornet*'s torpedo squadron 8, their defending Zeros were brought down so low that the American SBD Dauntless dive-bombers from the *Enterprise*, under the command of Wade McClusky, were able to attack with almost no opposition. It did not take long before three of the Japanese carriers, including the *Akagi*, *Kaga*, and *Soryu*, were either crippled, abandoned, or going up in flames. Meanwhile, the carrier *Hiryu* had managed to sink *Yorktown*, though aircraft from the *Enterprise* turned and did its best to sink *Hiryu* in response, setting her ablaze and damaging an accompanying destroyer, the *Isokaze*. Admiral Spruance then launched attacks against the Japanese cruisers *Mogami* and *Mikuma*, eventually managing to destroy them as well. The Japanese did not know it yet, but the U.S. had as good as won the battle.

As the battle progressed, the Japanese carriers quickly realized that they were falling behind. The logistics of simultaneously sending a second wave of bombers to Midway, avoiding the attacking U.S. aircraft, and trying to launch an airborne offensive against the newly-sighted U.S. Naval forces was too much for the carriers that were left. Defeated and appalled by their staggering losses, the Japanese began a general retirement by the night of June 4th-5th, turning their backs on Midway and officially retreating by the end of June 6th.

The Battle of Midway later marked a turning point in the war, because it signified a transition of power from Japan to the United States. Having clearly won the battle, the American forces retired while the Japanese returned to their homeland to lick their wounds. It had been six months to the day since the Japanese attacked Pearl Harbor, and now the Japanese Imperialist Empire had lost command of the Pacific Theater.

Admiral Yamamoto predicted that the Japanese would only last for another six months to a year after the attack at Pearl Harbor, and he was exactly correct. The U.S. Navy had officially overwhelmed Japan's fleet, signifying that the war in the Pacific was over.

The German Surrender at Stalingrad

In spite of the success of the U.S. in the Pacific and rapidly deteriorating Axis conditions, Germany and Japan would not give up the war willingly. In fact, they believed that until they were entirely out of options, they still had a chance of winning the war. Thus, it was another six months of determined fighting from both sides before disaster struck the German forces in a manner which they could not control; the weather.

While the Japanese were retreating from their defeat in the Pacific, Hitler launched an offensive against the USSR on June 22, 1941, despite the terms of the Nazi-Soviet Pact of 1939. Though the Red Army was significantly larger than the German army, Germany's superior air force and well-trained soldiers were able to fight them back across the Russian plains, inflicting severe damage on the Red Army and bringing ruin to the Soviet population as well. Incredibly, with the assistance of some troops from their Axis allies, Germany managed to overwhelm a vast amount of the USSR and made it all the way to Leningrad and Moscow by mid-October of 1941.

With General Paulus leading the offensive in the summer of 1942, the German troops raced to invade and destroy Stalingrad, per Hitler's orders. By August, the German Sixth Army had crossed the Volga River, while the German Fourth Air Fleet bombed Stalingrad and reduced it to rubble, resulting in the death of over 40,000 civilians. Then, in early September,

General Paulus and his troops reached Stalingrad at last, and Paulus launched his first direct offensives into the city. At the time, Paulus estimated that it would take his troops about ten days to capture Stalingrad. Little did he know that he was about to witness one of the most horrific, yet significant, battles of World War II.

Using a method not yet officially adopted into war strategy, both Germany and the USSR took the ruined city of Stalingrad to their advantage, making defensive fortifications out of the city's destroyed buildings and rubble. In a brutal and intense form of street fighting that the Germans called *Rattenkrieg*, or "Rat's War," the opposing forces broke into teams of eight or ten strong, fighting individually for every square inch of territory. Another devastating aspect of this street fighting was the new technology developed to comply with the street tactics, which included a German machine gun that could shoot blindly around corners, and a small Russian plane that could swoop low and quiet over German positions at night, dropping bombs without any warning. Before long, both sides were running low on water, food, medical supplies, and sleep. With each side suffering from endless casualties, tens of thousands perished every day. Then, when the cruelty of this war had finally reached its climax, the weather turned for the worst, leaving the Germans especially suffering from their greater lack of supplies and reinforcements. The war had reached a stalemate, and it would take a serious offensive to end the horrors of this terrible battle once and for all.

On November 19, the Soviets did just that. Beginning with a massive artillery bombardment, the Soviets launched a considerable counteroffensive against the Germans out of the rubble of Stalingrad. Led by General Zhukov and Soviet leader Joseph Stalin, after whom the city was named, the Soviets' attack was far greater than the Germans expected at such a late stage in battle, especially considering their own weakened position. Quickly overwhelming the Sixth Army with their offensive, which included 500,000 Soviet troops, 900 tanks, and 1,400 aircraft, the Soviets were able to surround the entire remaining German force, which at that point amounted to about 200,000 men. The Germans were defenseless and out of options, but still the Italian and Romanian troops at Stalingrad were the only ones to surrender. While the Germans waited for reinforcements and received limited supplies by air, Hitler demanded that they hold their position, saying, "The 6th Army will hold its positions to the last man and the last round." In order to ensure that his orders were followed, Hitler promoted Von Paulus to field marshal, knowing that no Nazi field marshal had ever surrendered and to do so would be a disgrace to the title. As the Russian winter descended and the Germans began to starve, more and more Germans were lost to frostbite, hypothermia, and starvation, which took as many lives as the ruthless Soviet troops. Finally, on January 21, 1943, the last of Germany's conquered airports fell to the Soviets, which meant that the Germans were officially on their own. There would be no reinforcements, there would be no more supplies, and finally, the Germans decided it was time to surrender. On the 31st of January, 1943, the southern sector of German forces surrendered, led by Von Paulus himself. By February 2nd, the rest of the troops surrendered. This ended one of the most pivotal battles in the history of World War II, and unofficially ended the battle on the European front. It was only a matter of time before the Second World War would have to come to an end.

Though Hitler was enraged that Von Paulus had chosen to surrender instead of committing an honorable suicide like he had been expected to do, there was not much Hitler could do.

By the end of the war, Von Paulus had repaid Hitler by selling out to the Soviets, joining the National Committee for Free Germany, and encouraging other German troops to surrender to the USSR. Meanwhile, of more than the 280,000 men under Paulus' command, only half were still alive by the time of surrender, with 35,000 soldiers evacuated from the front and the rest, about 91,000 soldiers, hauled off to Soviet prisoner of war camps. Unfortunately, only 5,000 of those troops would make it back to Germany after spending the rest of the war in the Soviet POW camps.

Hiroshima Bomb

In spite of the inevitable surrender of the German army and end to war on the European front, the Japanese had other plans. With a culture of honor and reward that hinged on success in battle, it was considered more honorable in Japanese culture for a soldier to give his life for the cause than to surrender. Thus, it was not an option for Japan to surrender with the Germans. In fact, to do so would be considered cowardly and would bring dishonor to the nation. Instead, they promised to fight until the very last; determined that fighting, even if it was fighting to their death, was the only option in war. Unfortunately, that also meant that the U.S. army and the Allies would suffer from severe casualties with the continuation of war, which is ultimately what led the U.S. leaders to make an unthinkable decision; to end the war, once and for all, by dropping an atomic bomb on Japan.

Even before the outbreak of war in 1939, several American scientists, many of whom were international immigrants and refugees from war, became fearful of Nazi Germany's research into nuclear weaponry. Determined not to be caught unawares by these new developments, the scientists approached the U.S. government in the hopes of beginning funding for a nuclear warfare program. In 1940, the U.S government agreed and began funding for a program to research and develop its own atomic weapons, which was under the joint responsibility of the Office of Scientific Research and Development and the War Department, due to the U.S.'s entry into World War II. Later, the U.S. Army Corps of Engineers spearheaded the construction of massive facilities for "The Manhattan Project," which was named for the engineering corps' Manhattan district and was a codename referring to the top-secret atomic weapons program. Following the development of the program, the scientists began research to produce key materials for nuclear fission; uranium-235 and plutonium (Pu-239). Once they discovered the materials they needed for creating nuclear fission, the scientists sent their research to Los Alamos, New Mexico, where a team led by J. Robert Oppenheimer worked to make an atomic bomb out of those materials. On the morning of July 16, 1945, at the Trinity test site in Alamogordo, New Mexico, the Manhattan Project managed its first successful test of an atomic weapon, a plutonium bomb. The atomic weapons project was a success, and it was only a matter of time before the scientists created a devastating atomic bomb of epic proportions that would wreak havoc on its target.

Meanwhile, Japan was holding strong to its belief in fighting to the death, refusing to admit defeat even while Axis forces in Europe surrendered. Even though Japan suffered severe casualties from war and American forces threatened closer to their homeland than ever before, they would not surrender. Then, between mid-April and mid-July of 1945, Japan inflicted serious damage on Allied forces, with casualties totaling nearly half of those suffered in three years of war in the Pacific. Unfortunately, Japan had only become more deadly in defeat, since its soldiers lost any hope of living through the war and willingly sacrificed themselves in suicide missions and bombing efforts. With this insane new level of violence, leaders in the U.S. deliberated the wisdom of continuing war with the Japanese, certain that Japan would cause unspeakable damage before the war was over. Additionally, even when the U.S. threatened to promptly and utterly destroy the Japanese if they refused to surrender, which was written and given to them in the Potsdam Declaration, Japan refused. Though some U.S. officials, like General Douglas MacArthur, believed that going through with "Operation Downfall," which was a considerable operation that would continue conventional bombing of Japan with a massive invasion following, other advisors believed that it was too late for conventional warfare tactics with the Japanese. If the U.S. hoped to defeat Japan without incurring the incredible casualties that typical warfare would inflict, which they tallied at about 1 million, then the U.S. would need to refer to an alternative option. Under this advising, newly-elected President Harry Truman decided, in spite of the moral reservations of Secretary of War Henry Stimson, General Dwight Eisenhower and a number of the Manhattan Project scientists, that it was time to put their nuclear developments to use. The decision made, Truman gave the order to drop the nation's newly-developed atomic bomb on Japan, and with that decision, determined the course of the end of World War II and postwar political dynamics.

On August 6th, 1945, a 9,000-pound uranium-235 bomb was loaded aboard a modified B-29 bomber at the U.S. base on the Pacific island of Tinian. The plane, piloted by Colonel Paul Tibbets and named *Enola Gay* after the pilot's mother, was headed for the U.S.'s number one target; Hiroshima. Chosen for its status as a manufacturing center with around 350,000 people and its location, which was about 500 miles away from Tokyo, Hiroshima was the ideal target for severely crippling Japan, as well as undermining the nation's morale.

The first atomic bomb, nicknamed "Little Boy," was dropped by parachute at 08.15 over Hiroshima the morning of August 6th. Exploding about 2,000 feet above Hiroshima with a blast that equaled 12-15,000 tons of TNT, "Little Boy" destroyed five square miles of the city and immediately killed 80,000 people, though thousands more would die from radiation exposure. In spite of this massive destruction, the bombing of Hiroshima failed to produce the response in the Japanese that it intended, and the nation refused to surrender. Thus, another atomic bomb was prepared to launch just three days later, Major Charles Sweeney dropped the second bomb, "Fat Man," on Nagasaki. Though the original target was supposed to be Kokura, thick clouds obscured Sweeney's view and he headed to Nagasaki instead, unloading "Fat Man" at 11.02 on the morning of the 9th. "Fat Man," weighing in at nearly 10,000 pounds and built to produce a 22-kiloton blast, was much larger than "Little Boy," though Nagasaki's topography limited the bomb's effect to a mere 2.6 square miles. While this bomb only killed 39,000 civilians, it was finally enough to convince Japan to unconditionally surrender. On August 15, 1942, Japan's Emperor Hirohito officially broadcasted Japan's surrender over the radio, citing the U.S.'s "new and most cruel bomb" as the cause, and effectively putting an end to World War II at last. This day would be forever consider "V-J Day," or the day that the Allied powers officially gained "Victory over Japan." It would be another few weeks, however, before Japan's formal surrender agreement was signed.

Conclusion

World War II lasted from September 1, 1939 until September 2, 1945, causing around 50-80 million deaths over the course of the war's six years. With the advance of western technology and weaponry, war had gained an unprecedented level of violence and death, and over 27,000 people were killed daily from start to finish. Sadly, 6 million of those deaths were Jewish civilians who died in the Holocaust during World War II. Because Hitler's plans for an Aryan race excluded the Jews, his anti-Semitic views led to the development of several concentration camps, with the main camps located at Dachau, Auschwitz, and Buchenwald. These camps put the Jews through excruciating torture and killed millions through inhumane means, which included death by gas showers, furnaces, medical experimentation, starvation, intense manual labor, firing squad, and many others. These unnecessary cruel tactics and the resulting devastation of the Jewish population is perhaps the greatest casualty that resulted from the Second World War.

Overall, this global war was fought between the Allied and Axis powers, with several nations representing each side. The Allied powers consisted of the U.S., led by Franklin D. Roosevelt; Russia, led by Joseph Stalin; Britain, led by Winston Churchill; China, led by Chiang Kai-shek; and France, led by Charles de Gaulle. The Axis powers included Germany, led by Adolf Hitler; Japan, led by Hirohito; and Italy, led by Benito Mussolini. The war began when Germany violated the Treaty of Versailles and invaded Poland, forcing France and Great

Britain to officially declare war. It did not end until after Japan surrendered, though Germany unconditionally surrendered on May 7th, 1945, a week after Hitler committed suicide. Japan did not officially surrender until their formal surrender agreement was signed on September 2, aboard the U.S. battleship, *Missouri*.

Though the war was officially over on September 2nd, it took several more years for the world to recover from the casualties and damage caused by the war. Many soldiers suffered from PTSD or were plagued by injuries that they would have for the rest of their lives, and several cities faced years of rebuilding and economic downturn. Memorials would also be established in locations around the world, celebrating the lives of those who bravely served their country and gave their lives for the cause. Politically, the United States and the USSR emerged from the war as global superpowers, which eventually pit them against each other in what would later become the Cold War.

While Adolf Hitler's leadership has been cited as the number one cause for World War II, it would be foolish to ignore the several other events which increased tensions and invited a return to war. Imperialist Japan was particularly guilty of increasing hostilities in Asia, since the nation invaded several areas of Asia and ultimately intended to assert its influence on the world. Additionally, mounting political unrest in Russia caused several civil wars, and the Communist party's eventual control of the nation led to later issues with the U.S. and other anti-Communist countries. Overall, it was the combination of several issues that led to World War II, which enforces the belief that there was no chance of avoiding another war.

Sources

U.S., Department of State, Publication 1983, Peace and War: United States Foreign Policy, 1931-1941 (Washington, D.C.: U.S., Government Printing Office, 1943), pp.3-8

https://ubcatlas.files.wordpress.com/2012/04/2004-mutter.pdf

https://www.mtholyoke.edu/acad/intrel/WorldWar2/manchuria.htm

http://apjjf.org/2012/10/37/Richard-J.-Smethurst/3825/article.html

https://www.quora.com/What-was-the-timeline-of-events-leading-up-to-WWII

https://www.britannica.com/event/World-War-II

https://www.ushmm.org/wlc/en/article.php?ModuleId=10005156

https://www.britannica.com/event/World-War-II/The-Battle-of-Britain

http://www.iwm.org.uk/history/8-things-you-need-to-know-about-the-battle-of-britain

http://www.history.com/news/10-things-you-should-know-about-the-battle-of-britain

https://www.britannica.com/event/Dunkirk-evacuation

https://www.archives.gov/publications/prologue/2011/winter/ph-decklogs.html

http://www.wtj.com/articles/pearl_harbor/

https://www.raf.mod.uk/history/bombercommandthethousandbomberraids3031may.cfm

http://research.calvin.edu/german-propaganda-archive/cologne.htm

https://www.britannica.com/event/Battle-of-Midway

http://www.molossia.org/milacademy/midway.html

http://www.history.com/this-day-in-history/germans-surrender-at-stalingrad

http://www.history.com/this-day-in-history/battle-of-stalingrad-ends

http://www.history.com/topics/world-war-ii/bombing-of-hiroshima-and-nagasaki

http://www.historynet.com/world-war-ii

Printed in Great Britain
by Amazon